LIFE IS A

STORY,

WRITE IT

JOYCE RILEY

i

DEDICATION

This book is humbly dedicated to those who wish to help others write their own life stories.

MEMORIES

Memories give us stories of the days of old.
Today is a story waiting to unfold.
Live it well and prayerfully,
And then write it carefully.

Write joyfully.
Write truthfully and know,
There is a power
In letting go.

LIFE IS A STORY, WRITE IT
Copyright 2015 Joyce Riley
ISBN 13: 978-1515232025
ISBN 10: 1515232026

LIFE IS A SONG

Life is a song. Sing it!
Life is a bell. Ring it!
Life is a candle. Light it!
Life is a book. Write it!
A song is no song until it is sung.
A bell is no bell until it is rung.
A candle won't glow until you light it.
Your book won't be read until you write it.

In musical terminology, a round is a short song which one person or group of people start singing and another group starts when the first group reaches the second phrase, as in, "Row, row, row your boat, gently down the stream. Merrily, merrily, merrily, merrily, life is but a dream." In using the analogy of life as a song I realized that life is a never ending round, with each generation adding to the song its own voice and its own interpretation. "And the Beat Goes On."

TABLE OF CONTENTS

CHAPTER ONE
GETTING STARTED

Stories, memoirs, tales of the past, call them what you will, memories matter. History paints a broad picture of world, national and local times and events but says little about the individuals who lived through those times: where they were, how they felt and how their lives were affected by local and world events. Not only have we lived through major historical times, we've made history of our own.

Don't you wish you knew more about your grandparents and great grandparents? Where did they come from? What were their homes like? How did they travel and how far did they go? What was it like in the kitchen? What was it like on the farm, in the mine, on the trail or in the king's or queen's parlor? What were their accomplishments, disappointments and aspirations?

Wouldn't you like to pick up a book or recording and have them answer your questions in their own words? Have you answered those questions for your children and grandchildren? If not, now is a good time to start.

If you like to work independently and are highly motivated, writing on your own may be your best choice; but, many people do better in a class environment, with guidelines and assignments to follow. Hearing other people's stories often creates 'ah ha' moments, leading to "I remember when—. "

Conducting Life Stories classes takes a lot of time and dedication but can be very rewarding and of service to others.

You don't need to be a teacher to be a Host. Interest and enthusiasm are what count most.

PUTTING IT INTO MOTION

WHERE TO MEET:

Once you have decided to form a class, you need a place to meet, one which doesn't charge for the use of the facilities. For small groups, (4 to 8), a private home can work well. For larger groups (8 to 16,) look for a room in your community's club house, a library, or local church. Twelve participants is an ideal number but I mention 16 because there are usually a few drop outs.

HOW TO ATTRACT PARTICIPANTS:

To attract people who are interested in writing their stories, talk about your interest. Let them see how enthused you are about writing and sharing. Advertise in your village paper, on a community web site, in church and library bulletins and newsletters.

LENGTH OF TIME

How long each class lasts will depend on how long you have the room and how many participants are attending. A small group meeting in a home will need less time than a larger group. Two hours is a comfortable length of time for most people. Ask people to keep their readings under 800 words, or about three minutes long, but be flexible.

HOW AND WHEN TO START

A starting time will depend, of course, on when you and a room are available. When talking to people who are interested ask for telephone numbers and E. mail addresses so you can contact them with the time, place and the date. Plan to meet once a week or, at least, every other week. People are usually anxious to share their stories but often forget or lose interest if meetings are too far apart.

MATERIAL NEEDED

Writing paper, pens or electronic note pads and, memories, desire and a text book.

Memories are like butterflies. You never know when one will light or how long it will stay. Capture them when you can.

There are many books available, which deal with memoirs writing. Since this teaching guide follows the path laid out in the book, "Life Is A Song, Sing It," it is highly recommended that participants use that book as a text. The "Memory Minders," will help stimulate their memories, the "Examples" will put their minds at rest, resulting in an "I can do that," attitude. And, they will be able to see what lies ahead.

GETTING STARTED

Welcome everyone; then read the poem "Life Stories" from "Life is a Song Sing It." It will help set a tone of trust for the class.

After passing around a signup sheet, stress the point that they are attending a writing, reading class, not a telling class.

As my former teacher said, "Write it, don't tell it." Many stories are told and then lost and forgotten. The written word has staying power.

Introduce yourself to the class (even if they know you) by reading a 'birth announcement', a 'who you are today' announcement, why you are writing and for whom you are writing.

Example:

My name is *Jane Smith*. I was born in Huston, Texas. My name is now *Jane Jones*. I'm married, live in Seattle, Washington in the summer and in Mesa, Arizona in the winter. I'm writing because there are so many stories I want to share with my children. I want them to know how things were, "back then."

By way of introductions, ask each member of the class to write and read their own announcements. Those announcements may sound boring but they will set the stage for the first assignment and get participants used to writing and reading out loud.

EFFECTIVE WRITING HINT

When writing a story, write or type on every other line. Skipping a line leaves room for corrections. If you are writing on a computer, save the old text. Sometimes first thoughts are the best thoughts. Read your story out loud, to yourself or to someone else; let it age.   Read it out loud again, then ask yourself, "Does it flow? Is it interesting? Is it honest?"

Often, when we are telling a story, we try to cram too much information into the tale. When possible, sketch only the back ground needed.

If other people are players in the scene explain their roles, not their history or your history with them. The people who are most important in your life deserve their own chapters in your book.

RESOURCES

What you remember and what someone else remembers may differ. Family members and long- time friends are wonderful resources. Comparing notes often shines a new light on an old memory. Don't forget, though, it's your story. Write what you remember, then add other versions.

PHOTOGRAPHS

A photo album can be a treasure trove of memories. Choose photographs which will help tell your story but remember, you are going to write your stories.

Make your book a book of stories with photographs, not another photo album with a few stories. That, of course is a matter of choice. Journals, old diaries and saved letters can be a treasure trove. For facts and figures look to:

LETTERS AND LEGAL DOCUMENTS
OLD NEWS PAPERS
COUNTY, STATE OR CITY RECORDS
OFFICES LIBRARIES, and of course
THE INTERNET

INTRODUCTIONS AND DEDICATIONS

A dedication and an introduction will help you keep focused on who you are writing for and why you are so bravely exposing your life and times to yourself and to others.

If you aren't sure how to get started on your introduction or dedication, check out some of your favorite autobiographies and see what other authors have written.

TITLES

Give each story a title. A title is like a road sign, which points in one direction or another and helps you stay on track. If you wish to change the title of your story when you are finished, do so.

SCENTS

Did someone in your family use a special perfume or smoke cigars? Do those smells remind you of the person you once knew? Did you like the smell? Did you like the person? For example: A favorite uncle smoked cigars, now every time I smell cigar smoke, I think of him. I don't like the smell but I like the memories it evokes.

As a child, did you wake up to the sweet smell of alfalfa and new mown hay or the not so sweet smell of chickens and cows?

Did you ever smell seaweed and fish as you stood by the sea? Do you remember the smells of buttered popcorn and bubble gum at the movie show?

Can you recall the scent of your grandmother's climbing rose, the smell of raindrops on asphalt or water from a hose?

COLORS

Did you have a favorite color? Do you have one now? What were the colors of your first house, the family car? What color was your mother's hair? Do you remember a stand of green trees, a blue lake, gray asphalt, a starlit night, or a cloth on the kitchen table, checkered red and white?

SOUNDS

Was your childhood filled with country sounds or city sounds? Do you remember the sound of music playing, of voices praying, air planes flying, babies crying, waves crashing, dishes smashing, the sound of trees falling, the voice your mother calling?

TASTES

Do you remember the taste of sour grass, cotton candy, strawberries from a mountain meadow, or the spoon full of sugar, which helped the medicine go down?

How many flavors of ice cream were sold at the general store? What was your favorite flavor? What foods did you like?

What foods did you hate? Did your mother always say, "Eat what's on your plate"?

TEXTURES/FEELINGS

Did you ever sit on a velvet chair or stroke your blanket or teddy bear? Did you like the feel of raindrops on your nose and mud between your toes? Did you pick up worms, snakes and frogs and lumpy, bumpy toads?

Did you like the feel of furry kittens, hate rough towels and woolen mittens? Could you feel the power in your hands when you gave your horse a new command? Were your father's hands smooth or rough? Did you ever feel the sting of a switch, a bump on your head, when you fell in a ditch? Was your bed too hard, just right, or too soft? Did you ever sleep in the hay in an old barn loft?

SIGHTS

Most of us live in a world of sight and take what we see for granted. Try, now, to recall some "first sights".

Do you remember the first time you saw a baby chick, a peacock or a monkey in the zoo, a lighted Christmas tree, burning candles or the bicycle, which was meant for you? Did you ever really look at your grandmother's old, old face? Did you ever take trips to see new places, strange tall buildings and foreign faces? Did you ever see an elephant fly or something so sad it made you cry?

EFFECTIVE WRITING HINT

Use quotes when you can. Comments or conversations quoted add interest and realism to a story. Life is not a solo event. Give others a voice.

EXAMPLES

THE DIRECT QUOTE:
Mother always said, "I love you," when she tucked me into bed.

THE PROBABLE QUOTE
I think it was Daddy who said, "Always tie you shoe laces before you start to walk."

THE IMAGINED QUOTE
As I started up the cliff, I could almost hear them say, "She'll never make it."

Read Chapter One of "Life Is A Song, Sing It" and Chapter Two, through page 19.

Once you've gathered your facts, write a birth announcement. Then weave it into a story.

CHAPTER TWO

WHAT'S IN A NAME?

Is there a story behind your name? Were you named after a relative, a family friend or, perhaps, a character in a novel? Is it a biblical name? Many name books give a meaning to each name. Do you know what it is?

Do you like your names? Have you changed a name, either through marriage or by choice? Did you have a nick name as a kid? Do you have one now?

Write a story about your name, or the history of your family name.

FIRST HOME

MEMORY MINDERS

Did your parents move from your first house before you were old enough to remember the move? Did you live in the country or in a city? Can you describe the first home you remember? Was it constructed of wood, stucco, or brick? Was it a one or two story house? Or, did you live in an apartment? What floor was the apartment on? Did your first home seem large or small?

How was the dwelling heated? Did it have a fireplace or wood burning stove? Did it have, perhaps, a steam radiator?

Do you remember the furniture in the living room or pictures on the walls? Describe your bedroom.

Did you share it with anyone? Are there any special colors, odors or sounds associated with your home? Did it have a squeaky floor, a rough-hewn door? Do you remember bacon frying, babies crying? What was dinner time like? Was there enough food to eat? What was your favorite treat?

How many people lived in your home? Were any special stories told about you as an infant or small child? What were your family dinners like? Who was your primary caretaker? Who did you feel most close to? How well did you get along with your siblings?

Do you have any lingering fears or special, loving memories associated with your early childhood? Who supported your family, monetarily and emotionally? What were your family's roots? Was adoption a factor in your life?

If so, describe what you know about the circumstances of the adoption or foster care. Did you go to church with the family? How did your family's religion influence your life? Do you remember the surroundings? Did you play stick ball in the street or have fields to roam in?

Choose from the above and write a story or two or three about your early years.

Write a story about a playmate, playtime or work time when you were a child.

KINDERGARTEN AND BEYOND MEMORY MINDERS

How old were you when you started school? Did you attend kindergarten or start in the first grade?

Were you excited or afraid to go to school? How did you get there? Had you visited the school with a parent, sister or brother? Did you make friends quickly? Were you a model child or was it hard to sit still? Where was the school located? Was it a one story or two story building? Did your room have a blackboard and erasers, or a white board and computers? Was there a cloakroom for hanging coats? Were you ever sent there for "time out?" What did it smell like?

What were your playground and after school activities? Did you go straight home? What were your after school chores? As you grew older, was there a special teacher counselor or mentor who made a difference in your young life?

Write a story about school days, your favorite or least favorite teacher.

TURNING POINTS

MEMORY MINDERS

Was a baby born? Did someone you love die? Was there an illness or accident involving you or a family member? Was moving to a new home or going to school or changing schools a major event, one which changed how you lived and felt? Did your family ever suffer through war or a natural disaster? Did someone encourage or discourage you in an endeavor? Were you ever a victim of brutality or molestation? If so, how was it handled?

Don't shy away from the bad stuff. It too, is a part of your life. You might choose to write it and then erase it.

Write about a turning point in your young life. Tell of its effect on you. Good or bad, tell it like it was.

MEMORY MINDERS

Do you remember trips you took as a child, illnesses, health care, medications and home remedies, family pets, family traditions, holidays and "every day" days? How do today's holiday traditions differ from when you were a child? What was the main source of entertainment of the time? Did you attend Saturday matinees, listen to the radio? Had the age of television begun? Do you remember what songs were popular?

Write a story or stories about your favorite holidays, your favorite form of entertainment, your favorite radio programs, movies or songs.

WHERE WERE YOU WHEN?

This is, perhaps, a good time to think about, "Where you were "when."

You may remember when Pearl Harbor was attacked, when President Roosevelt died. Many readers will remember where they were when John F. Kennedy and Martin Luther King were assassinated. Even more will remember where they were when the Twin Towers fell.

Be selective when you write. Write about what interests you most or what you think your family will be most interested in. Don't forget to write about the life and times around you. Tell your readers what you saw what you heard and how you felt.

Write a story about, "Where you were—When."

HAPPIER MEMORIES

Many of us had pets when we were growing up. Did you have a favorite pet or pets as a child? What were they? And what were their names?

Did your children grow up with pets in the home? Do you still have a pet to help keep you company?

Write a story about your favorite pet or pets.

LESSONS LEARNED

Life is full of lessons and,
With every lesson learned,
Another door is opened,
Another corner turned.

From the following list choose a subject and write about a skill learned. Who taught you? Did you learn on your own? How did you feel then and how do you feel now about your accomplishment?

How, when and where did you learn to:

Ride a bicycle, roller skate, in-line skate, skateboard,

Make a scooter, bake a pie, multiply, spell Mississippi,

Ride a horse, drive a tractor, drive a car, change a flat tire,

Shave, put on make-up, swim, water ski, snow ski, snow board,

Use a power tool, use a computer, play an instrument,

Speak another language, dance, play a card game.

Fly a kite, fly an airplane?

Add your accomplishments to this list and learn something new today. Using at least some of Kipling's six, honest men, (Where, and What and When and Why and How and Who,) write a story about something you were proud to have accomplished, someone who encouraged you to follow your dream.

CHAPTER THREE

COMING OF AGE

In writing about your childhood years you followed a time line. Now, as you approach the subject of your teen years, you will find many branches and turning points, many choices offered and made. Many cultures celebrate a child's coming of age. For some it's a Bar or Bat Mitzvah. For others a Quinceanera, a sweet sixteen party, or a coming out party, a scouting award. For some, "coming of age" meant, "a driver's license."

Write a Coming of Age story.

By the time you reached sixteen years of age you were old enough to drive a car and hold down an after school job.

You were probably living life forward, sideways and up-side down.

Write about a summer job or school activity.

For example:

"The Jobs I Held While in School."
"From Sixteen to Eighteen, in a Souped-Up Car,"
 "Sewing Costumes for the Drama Class,"
"On the Playing Field."
"On the Sidelines."
"On the Road With Family of Friends."

MORE CHOICES

You had many choices then and you have choices now. You can continue to write chronologically, or you can focus on subject matter by following one subject through a lengthy period of time.

For example: You could write about your first job, the careers and career changes, which followed.

You could write about your first car, your favorite car, racing cars, fixing cars, selling cars, cars then and now.

MORE HIGH SCHOOL MEMORY MINDERS

Was your senior year exciting or stressful? Were you preparing for college or a career? Did you drop out of school? If so, what did you do? Did you get a job, join the military, travel?

At school, did you hold a student body office? Did you sing in a choir, or play an instrument in a band? Did you attend the senior prom and grad night?

How did you feel about leaving high school, your teachers and your friends?

Write what you would like others to know about your expectations for the future.

AND THE BEAT GOES ON

What musical groups were you listening to when you were in your teens and early twenties? What were your favorite songs? Who was your favorite singer?

Write a story about the music you grew up with.

AFTER GRADUATION
MEMORY MINDERS

Where did you go and what did you do when you left high school?

Did you go directly to college, into the military or to work? Did you move from the family home, have a room- mate, travel? Were you prepared to handle your own finances? Were you prepared to be out on your own? Why did you choose the college, job or branch of service you went into?

Write a story about where you went or what you did when you left school.

AN EFECTIVE WRITING HINT

Relax! Don't become tense while writing. But, at the same time, watch your tenses (past, present, future).

LOOKING BACK AT LOOKING BACK

Let's review some of the reasons we're writing our life stories. First, we want to leave a personal history of our lives and times for future family members. They may not show an interest now but life changes quickly from generation to generation. At some point in the future someone will be grateful for this look into the past.

Think of your readers as you write. Ask yourself if what you are writing will be of interest in years to come.

Think of what you wish you had asked your parents or grandparents. Now, ask these questions of yourself and include the answers in your book.

Including local and world events and how they affected you will give future readers a greater insight into your life and times. Don't just think or write about the past.

Write about today's events while they are still fresh in your mind. Report what is happening and how you are feeling.

Has a recent event changed your outlook on life? Did it make you happy, sad, angry or more appreciative of what you have? Beyond writing for our families, we are writing for ourselves. We don't want to live in our memories but to learn from them and, perhaps see others and ourselves in a more understanding light.

CHAPTER FOUR
YOUNG ADULTHOOD
GETTING ESTABLISHED

MEMORY MINDERS

By the ripe age of twenty five, most of us had established careers and/or a marriage and, ready or not, had become parents.
Do you remember your first "real" job, your first "real" love? How old were you when you said, "I do?" Was your wedding large or small? Who planned your wedding? Did you go on a honeymoon? Have you ever gone on a belated honeymoon?

Write about your career plans, your wedding plans or your baby plans.

AROUND AND AROUND WE GO

Following the outline of your childhood, write about your children's 'birth days' and early years. Better still, do a story album for each child. Include photos and memories of family vacations, holidays and everyday life. Recall your children's triumphs and disappointments and how you shared in them.

Remind them of the days when you watched little league games, dance recitals, swim meets, etc. Include many "parent" activities in which you were involved. Remind them of the worry you felt when they started to drive and the relief you felt when they came home on time and alive. If you were a working dad or mom, tell your children about the challenges of juggling the responsibilities of work and home. Today, they may be experiencing many of those challenges themselves.

Write a health history for each of your children. While you are at it, write your own health history, including then and now. And, if you haven't already done so, consider drafting a Living Trust and writing a Living Will.

Keep your children informed. Share your fond memories with them and ask them to share their memories with you.

CHAPTER FIVE
MIDDLE AGE (?)

Bracketed by youth and age, the middle years took up many years of our lives. We chose mates, left or lost mates, established careers, and left or lost careers. We raised children, became grandparents and often took care of our parents. The middle years served up great possibilities and many responsibilities.

MEMORY MINDERS

As you reached "middle age" you probably found yourself facing more dramatic changes and choices.

Did you buy a new home, build a new home, move across the country?

If you had children, how were they impacted by the changes?

Did your children or parents influence some of your decisions? Did you face financial ups and downs? Were there marital problems? Did you "come out of the closet" or choose a different life style? How did your parents, children and society accept your decisions?

**Choose one of the above
and write from the heart.**

MORE ABOUT THE MIDDLE YEARS

During the middle years many people either move on or take on new responsibilities. Children grow, parents age.

Did you suffer from, 'the empty nest syndrome', fall into 'the sandwich years', dealing with growing children and aging parents?

Did graduations, weddings and doctor's appointments fill your calendar? If you have children, when did you first become a grandparent?

Write about a child leaving the nest, becoming a grandparent and/or making room for more.

CHAPTER SIX

RETIRED AND RE-INSPIRED

Retired is defined, in Webster's Thesaurus, as "handed down," "withdrawn," "secluded." Few of the retired people I know are secluded or withdrawn. Many are pursuing new careers, new or old hobbies. Some retirees are traveling. Many are doing volunteer work. Perhaps they are writing their life stories. Some people are doing it all. This is not to say that retirement doesn't take an attitude adjustment.

MEMORY MINDERS

Were you financially and mentally prepared for "retirement"? If you were married did one of you retire before the other? What adjustments did that entail? Did you have plans for retirement?

Like every other stage in our lives, retirement is a time to make adjustments, accept changes and meet challenges.

Were you prepared for retirement, financially, emotionally? Did one partner retire before the other? How did he or she adjust to the change? Did you make a bold move? Start traveling? Did you "hit the road?" Start a new hobby, renew an old hobby? Did you start a new career or go back to school?

Write a retirement story.

CHAPTER SEVEN

The Olden Years

MEMORY MINDERS

How do you know when you are old? Well----

-

You're really old if you remember penny post cards, phone booths, (ten cents a call) and an operator asking, "Number please."

You know you're getting old when your hair starts turning grey—in places where you never had hair before. ("Like in your ears, Grandma?")

You're old if you can remember going to a Saturday matinee (two features, news, a serial, a cartoon and buttered popcorn) for a quarter; and if you remember how hard you worked for that quarter.

You know you are getting old if you can't remember where you put your glasses or if you took your morning pills today.

But you do remember when your mother fed you castor oil and put a mustard plaster on your chest.

You're old if your family had a two party telephone line and the mailman came to your mailbox rain or shine.

You know you are getting old when your kids start receiving The AARP magazine.

If your memories say you are old, be thankful for being old and for remembering when, and how life was "way back then."

Write about how you feel about your age.

LETTER WRITING and JOURNALING

It's a lot easier to keep current than to go back and try to remember. But, in our enthusiasm for writing about yesteryears we often forget last month, last week, today. These present moments are all a part of tomorrow's past.

JOURNAL = a daily record of occurrences or observations.

Many of us keep journals when we travel. We do this because we want to remember and relive the journey. But every day is a journey. Whether written daily, weekly, or monthly, a journal gives us a tool for reviewing the 'who', 'when', and 'where' of our lives. Our stories will add the 'how' and the 'why'.

CHAPTER EIGHT

PUTTING IT ALL TOGETHER

It's time to re-read your stories, edit them and tighten them. It is also time to decide if you really want to share what you have written. Ask yourself, "Will someone be hurt by what I have written?" If the answer is, "yes," keep it to yourself.

Now, put what you are going to publish in the order you have chosen and make chapter headings. Since you know what you have written, it's easy to miss mistakes, so enlist a friend or two to critique and edit what you have composed.

This is also a good time to go through family photos and choose pictures that will illustrate your stories or chapters. And, if you haven't already done so, write an introduction and/or dedication.

One meaning for the word, dedicate, as defined in Webster's dictionary is: to address or inscribe (a book, artistic performance, etc.) to someone as a sign of honor or affection. An introduction, in my words, tells them what you are going to tell them.

If you aren't sure how to get started on your introduction or dedication, check out some of your favorite autobiographies and see what other authors have written. But, don't be afraid to be original.

WHAT'S NEXT?

Or, maybe what's first if you decided to enter your text into the computer to get ready to publish. Check out www.createspace.com to learn about any formatting suggestions for their particular publishing system. There are minimum margins required; so set them up first.

And, you need to decide what size book you want to end up with before you start typing in Word. This book's Trim size and Page size in Word 5.5" x 8.5".

There are other books published about all of the details and rules to be followed to make it easier to update and make changes.

This book was prepared using Microsoft Word. Editing help is also available from many 'do-it-yourself' publishing companies. Front Cover and Back Cover design help is also available if needed.

Made in the USA
Middletown, DE
26 July 2022

69993655R00033